# Theos Friends' Progra

CW00393025

Theos is a religion and society think tank which seeks opinion about the role of faith and belief in society.

We were launched in November 2006 with the suppo Dr Rowan Williams and the Cardinal Archbishop of W Cardinal Cormac Murphy-O'Connor.

## We provide

- high-quality research, reports and publications;
- an extensive events programme;
- news, information and analysis to media companies, parliamentarians and other opinion formers.

## We can only do this with your help!

Theos Friends receive complimentary copies of all Theos publications, invitations to selected events and monthly email bulletins.

Theos Associates receive all the benefits of Friends and in addition are invited to attend an exclusive annual dinner with the Theos Director and team.

If you would like to become a Friend or an Associate, please visit www.theosthinktank.co.uk or detach or photocopy the form below, and send it with a cheque to Theos for the relevant amount. Thank you.

Yes, I would like to help change public opinion!
I enclose a cheque payable to Theos for: ☐ **£60** (Friend) ☐ **£300** (Associate)
Other amount_____

☐ Please send me information on how to give by direct debit

Name_____

Address _____

_____

_____ Postcode _____

Email _____

Tel _____

*Theos will use your personal information to keep you updated about its activities. Theos will not pass your details to any third party to be used for marketing activities. If you wish to change the way we communicate with you please phone us on 02078287777. Theos sub-contracts its data processing. Our data processing contractors are bound by the terms of this statement.*

*Please return this form to:*
Theos | 77 Great Peter Street | London | SW1P 2EZ
S: 97711 D: 36701

# Theos

## Theos – clear thinking on religion and society

Theos is a Christian think tank working in the area of religion, politics and society. We aim to inform debate around questions of faith and secularism and the related subjects of values and identity. We were launched in November 2006, and our first report *'Doing God': a Future for Faith in the Public Square,* written by Nick Spencer, examined the reasons why faith will play an increasingly significant role in public life.

## what Theos stands for

In our post-secular age, interest in spirituality is increasing across western culture. We believe that it is impossible to understand the modern world without an understanding of religion. We also believe that much of the debate about the role and place of religion has been unnecessarily emotive and ill-informed. We reject the notion of any possible 'neutral' perspective on these issues.

## what Theos works on

Theos conducts research, publishes reports and runs debates, seminars and lectures on the intersection of religion, politics and society in the contemporary world. We also provide regular comment for print and broadcast media. Research areas include religion in relation to public services, the constitution, law, the economy, pluralism and education.

## what Theos provides

In addition to our independently driven work, Theos provides research, analysis and advice to individuals and organisations across the private, public and not-for-profit sectors. The Theos team have extensive experience in quantitative, qualitative and ethnographic research and consultancy. For more information about Theos Consultancy contact the team at hello@theosthinktank.co.uk.

## what Theos believes

Theos was launched with the support of the Archbishop of Canterbury and the Cardinal Archbishop of Westminster, but it is independent of any particular denomination. We are an ecumenical Christian organisation, committed to the belief that religion in general and Christianity in particular has much to offer for the common good of society as a whole. We are committed to the traditional creeds of the Christian faith and draw on social and political thought from a wide range of theological traditions. We also work with many non-Christian and non-religious individuals and organisations.

# The Church and the Charter
## Christianity and the forgotten roots of the Magna Carta

Thomas Andrew

Foreword by Larry Siedentop

Published by Theos in 2015
© Theos

ISBN 978-0-9574743-8-3

Theos
Licence Department
77 Great Peter Street
London
SW1P 2EZ

T 020 7828 7777
E hello@theosthinktank.co.uk
www.theosthinktank.co.uk

# contents

# foreword

This is a refreshing essay. For it runs against some of the prejudices of our time. Today identifying and reclaiming the Christian part of our heritage is an important challenge. Why, for example, has asking about the Christian sources of Magna Carta been so rare? Indeed, why has there been so little attempt to relate the development of European political ideas generally with the development of Christian theology and morals? There are, I suppose, a number of reasons.

The professionalizing of intellectual life, with an ever-increasing division of labour, is one reason. Taking for granted a distinction between the secular and sacred spheres has made it easy to push study of the latter to one side. That inclination has been reinforced by an assumption that the two spheres have and perhaps should have little to do with each other – that they are, so to speak, natural enemies. Yet that is a paradoxical view because the distinction between the secular and sacred was first made and defended by the church.

The need felt by the church in the 11th and 12th century to defend itself from threats to its autonomy posed by emergent feudalism led to important innovations in the thought and practice of the church. It led to the creation of a more systematic canon law and a radical new emphasis on the importance of legal procedure for a 'just outcome'. And not only that. The understanding of justice itself began to be more closely associated with the assumption of moral equality. For a strong case can be made that the earliest form of natural rights theory was the work of canon lawyers from the 12th to the 14th century – lawyers who transformed the idea of natural law inherited from the ancient world, by giving it a far more individualist cast. In their hands, 'aristocratic' liberty, liberty understood as personal and corporate privileges, began to give way to a more 'democratic' conception of liberty.

The virtue of the present essay is that it seeks to lodge the formation of Magna Carta against this larger background. The essay does not ignore or seek to minimize the role of circumstances – the conflicts between kings, barons and prelates arising from their different ambitions and interests. Yet neither does it ignore the larger intellectual background at a period when European thought was largely shaped by churchmen, and it finds important traces of their influence in Magna Carta. The influence of Canterbury especially figured in both the formation and preservation of Magna Carta. So it should be no surprise that the liberties of the church are asserted at its very outset.

Today there is a widespread embarrassment about confronting the role of the Christian church in the formation of the Western world. The Western debt to ancient Greece and Rome is far more likely to be emphasized than its debt to Christian moral thought. Yet there is a strong case to be made that our conception of society and of a just legal system cannot be fully understood apart from that debt. When we ignore it, we fail to understand ourselves.

Larry Siedentop is the author of *Inventing the Individual: The Origins of Western Liberalism* (Allen Lane, 2014)

# acknowledgement

Thanks must go to The Fairfield Trust and the Howard Garrood Fund for their grants towards the publication of this report. The list of Magna Carta scholars whose work I have drawn upon is a long one, but I am particularly indebted to Professor Nicholas Vincent of the University of East Anglia, whose work on the life and thought of Stephen Langton was invaluable. I also owe a great debt of gratitude to all the team at Theos, but particularly to Alanna Harris, for her support during my time there, and to Nick Spencer, for reading and commenting on early drafts of this report.

# introduction

*Magna Carta is the greatest constitutional document of all times – the foundation of the freedom of the individual against the arbitrary authority of the despot.*

Lord Denning[1]

For those familiar with the plaudits but unfamiliar with the text, an initial reading of the Magna Carta can be a somewhat underwhelming experience. Where one might expect to find bold assertions of human liberty in the face of royal tyranny, we are instead confronted with a range of technical and occasionally obscure royal concessions governing all manner of everyday matters – from tax and inheritance to forestry practice and the location of fish weirs. Such trivial points of law can be difficult to reconcile with our perception of the Magna Carta as a document that, as Barack Obama recently put it, "first laid out the liberties of man."[2] Heralded as the foundation of good government, of democracy, of the United States Declaration of Independence, and of the Universal Declaration of Human Rights, no other document in history carries such a burden of expectation based on so little an obvious contribution.

In part, this is because the Magna Carta has enjoyed an almost totemic status amongst politicians and lawmakers since first being issued in the 13th century. And as with any such document, great liberties have been taken with its interpretation and application. This was particularly true during the parliamentary struggle against the absolutist claims of the Stuart monarchs in the 17th century, when the Magna Carta was upheld as a guarantee of individual liberty and as a damning indictment against the sovereignty of the king, but it also remains true today. In his closing speech at the Conservative Party conference in 2014, Prime Minister David Cameron had a word for the European Court's

*"This is the country that wrote the Magna Carta… we do not need lecturing… from judges in Strasbourg."*

contentious interpretation of human rights. "This is the country that wrote the Magna Carta… we do not need lecturing on this from judges in Strasbourg."[3]

When we look closely at the text however, we can see that this totemic status is not simply the product of historical fiction and fluke circumstance. Rather, the Magna Carta assumes its place in the canon of intellectual political history because it is the greenhouse in which certain ideas about the individual and the state were first allowed to germinate. This is not to say that our modern concepts about liberty and right are in any way synonymous with those half-formed notions that spread their shallow roots just under the surface of the text. Rather, it is to say that these ideas about what constituted just action on the part of the governing authority are the genesis of the more fully developed, more cogent and coherent theories of liberty and right that modern political thought attributes to the individual. It is in the Magna Carta that we first see, enshrined in law, the demand for due process within the judicial system. It is in the Magna Carta that we first see limitations placed on the monarch as someone answerable to the law. And it is in the Magna Carta that we first see rights language extended to "all free men", rather than restricted to an elite group.

This essay is not concerned with how these ideas came to lay the foundations of future rights language. Rather, the concern to be addressed here is how these initial ideas came to be enshrined, half-formed and often obscured, within "The Great Charter of the Liberties of England". There are, of course, a myriad of influencing factors, and not all of noble origin. The barons who extracted the charter from King John had their own interests and their own agendas to preserve. So too did Stephen Langton, the Archbishop of Canterbury who was so influential in negotiating the contents of the Charter. But it would be too simplistic to stop there – to imagine that the ideas that we find in the Magna Carta are nothing more than a reactionary response to a vindictive and over-reaching king.

> *No account of the Magna Carta can be complete without reference to the Church.*

A more nuanced position recognises that the ideas contained within the Magna Carta are part of a developing intellectual tradition. They did not emerge *ex nihilo*, but arose as an expression of pre-existing thought, given shape and substance in the political demands of the moment. And a key aspect of that intellectual tradition is the contribution of the Christian Church and Christian theology.

No account of the Magna Carta can be complete without reference to the Church. Indeed, given the prominence placed on the principle of ecclesiastical liberty within the text, no account of the Magna Carta should even *begin* without acknowledging the Church's role in its formation. And yet popular thinking seems all too willing to ignore it altogether. While academic scholarship has produced some notable studies into the theological background of the Archbishop of Canterbury, material aimed at the general public has largely failed to recognise the contribution of Christian theology or the Church in the formation of the Magna Carta. When the British Library ran a series of events exploring the 800 year-old roots of 'Britain's struggle for freedom and rights',[4] the contribution of the Church was all but ignored. And as the professor of political science Cary Nederman points out, while commentators will often pay lip service to the principles of ecclesial liberty enshrined in the first clause of the Magna Carta, this is generally done with the attitude of someone fulfilling a formal requirement, before they can move on to the meatier parts of the text.[5]

There are two problems here. The first is that to fail to address the vital role played by the Church in both the build-up to the Magna Carta and the events that followed, is to miss a crucial part of the Magna Carta's story. This is particularly true of the Archbishop of Canterbury, who was instrumental not only in negotiating the Charter of 1215, but also in the important reissue of 1225 under Henry III, which confirmed the Magna Carta's place in history. Perhaps more important than this, however, is that a failure to acknowledge the Christian theological context within which the Magna Carta arose is to miss out on an understanding of some of the most important roots of our political and intellectual heritage.

> *A failure to acknowledge the Christian theological context within which the Magna Carta arose is to miss out on an understanding of some of the most important roots of our political and intellectual heritage.*

This essay will seek to redress the imbalance in two ways. Firstly, it will seek to place the practical role of the Christian Church right at the heart of the Magna Carta story. For while King John's struggle with the barons might have taken up many of the headlines, there is a second historical narrative that runs parallel to the first. This relates to King John's turbulent and multi-faceted relationship with the English Church, and is a narrative that proves just as vital as the first to the Magna Carta's creation and continued prosperity. Second, this essay will assess the theological context of late 12th and early 13th century England, within which the Magna Carta arose, and look at how key themes that occur in the Magna Carta were reflective of many of the theological ideas of the day.

Before we can look at the contribution of the Church in any great detail, however, we must first understand the broader story of the Magna Carta. And for this, we must turn to King John himself.

# introduction – references

1   Danny Danziger and John Gillingham, *1215: The Year of Magna Carta* (New York: Touchstone, 2003), p. 268.

2   http://www.bbc.co.uk/news/uk-politics-13549927

3   http://www.politicshome.com/uk/article/105662/david_cameron_speech_to_2014_conservative_party_conference.html

4   http://www.bl.uk/takingliberties

5   Cary Nederman, "The Liberty of the Church and the Road to Runnymede: John of Salisbury and the Intellectual Foundations of the Magna Carta" in *PS: Political Science and Politics*, Vol. 43, No. 3 (July 2010), p. 458.

# the road to Runnymede

## bad King John

While doubts remain as to whether the King John made famous by Robin Hood is an entirely justified caricature, the general scholarly consensus is that he was neither a nice man nor a particularly effective ruler. As vindictive and licentious as his brother and father before him, John also proved to be untrustworthy and arrogant. Lacking both the military instincts of his brother Richard and the political tact of his father Henry, he eventually brought England to civil war and the brink of financial ruin.

The sins of King John are too numerous to go into here in any great detail. However, it is worth noting one broad theme which characterised much of his kingship, and which is particularly important for understanding the context within which baronial opposition and eventually the Magna Carta arose. This relates to the arbitrary way with which John sought to impose his royal will, showing little regard for due process, custom or basic principles of fairness. His main concern was to increase the revenues at his disposal and, as sovereign, John had the tools to do so ready to hand.

A key tool in this regard was the judicial system, which had gone through a period of significant change under Henry II. By establishing the 'eyres' – groups of semi-professional judiciaries who travelled across England dispensing the king's justice – King Henry II had sought to take legal decision-making under royal control, and out of the hands of the barons and lords. The reforms had proven immensely popular, and land-holders of all social status came to have their case heard at the king's courts.

While this new system was undoubtedly an improvement on the old, it also facilitated a dramatic increase in the scope and power of the monarchy. It was particularly useful as a source of revenue for the royal purse, with justices able to charge large fees on the king's behalf. By the time of King John, and with a Treasury close to bankruptcy, these fees not only became more and more exorbitant, they also became more and more suspect. Bribery and corruption became an integral part of the medieval court, particularly when it came to land disputes. Litigants would offer far higher fees in return for a favourable verdict, while some would simply offer enormous amounts of money to bypass the judicial system altogether. [1]

It wasn't simply within the judiciary that King John began to exercise such liberties however. Professor of Medieval History Nicholas Vincent paints a picture of a king who was petty, vindictive, and acted on a cruel whim with regards to even his most trusted courtiers. The court of King John was a royal court "consumed by angst and racked with paranoia".[2] Extortionate demands were extracted at every possible turn, regardless of whether those being made to pay could afford it. When Geoffrey de Mandeville, Earl of Essex, bid to marry the former queen, Isabella of Gloucester (married to King John before he was granted an annulment by the Pope in 1199), John forced him to pay a fine of 20,000 marks, an exorbitant sum of money.[3] This fine, coupled with the fact that John kept most of Isabella's lands for himself, left Geoffrey with a debt that would endure for several generations, costing him and his descendants a vast portion of their lands and estates.

In addition to the corruption of John's judiciary, and to the extortionate fines which he levied on the nobles within his court, a key aspect in fermenting unrest among the aristocracy at the excesses of royal power was the king's use of taxation – specifically against the tenants who held his lands under the feudal system. John demanded scutage payments from his tenants eleven times in just seventeen years – compared to the eleven times it had been demanded during the reigns of the three preceding monarchs combined. Scutage was intended to exempt a knight or baron from waging war on the king's behalf, but it seems that John began to use it in an arbitrary fashion, regardless of whether he ever actually intended to go to war. Further taxes and charges levied on tenants included a dramatic increase in the charges placed on widows who wished to remain single and thus keep their deceased husbands' lands, a radical extension of the fines relating to the use of the king's forests (accompanied by a large increase in the number and powers of local sheriffs to enforce the king's forest laws), and a brand new tax on moveable goods, introduced in 1207.[4]

*Of those who lost out under John's rule, it was the Northern barons who were hit hardest.*

All these extra taxes, combined with the corruption of the Royal Court, did not make for a very easy political environment. And of those who lost out under John's rule, it was the Northern barons who were hit hardest, as the king sought to re-appropriate powers that had been lost to the North during the turbulent years of the 12th century. However, it wasn't until 1212 that events started to come to a head.

# baronial opposition

In 1212, rumours began to circulate of a baronial plot to murder the king. The alleged conspirators, Robert fitz Walter and Eustace de Vescy, both fled into exile, but the allegations brought John's tensions with the barons to the fore. The most notable outcome of this escalation was John's appeal to the Pope, in the spring of 1213. Declaring England and Ireland to be papal fiefdoms, John subjected himself and his lands, not only to papal authority, but also to papal protection. Having waged a battle of wills with the Church for much of his reign (a battle to which we will later turn), King John now placed himself under her wings.

As a political gamble, the move could have been a masterstroke. The barons were now forced to direct their demands to the Pope, who had a vested interest in preserving the integrity of monarchical sovereignty. But John, perhaps emboldened by the papal protection he now enjoyed, redoubled his efforts at enhancing the wealth of the English treasury. It was during this period that many of the most exorbitant fines of King John (including the 20,000 marks demanded from Gregory de Mandeville) were recorded, and some of the most frequent and excessive demands for scutage made.

John was not simply acting on a whim, however. He had long been obsessed with the idea of retaking the Norman lands he had lost so spectacularly in the early years of his reign. In 1214, he set out at the head of his army to Poitou, where he intended to fight northwards and join up with the rest of his forces who had been fighting in France since the winter. On 27th July, however, shortly after John had arrived in Poitou, his northern army suffered a devastating defeat at Bouvines. John was forced to return to England utterly crushed: his armies were depleted and the country's finances were in tatters.

The political impact of the defeat at Bouvines was immediate. While a number of the northern barons had refused to pay John scutage or send forces for his attack on France, open dissent seems to have been relatively rare. The invasion of France had been attempted on an enormous scale, and would certainly have required at least limited baronial support. With the decimation of his armies and the total failure to reclaim Norman lands, however, what support John did have quickly faded away. And as an ever greater number of barons decided to throw their lot in with their disaffected peers, his position became increasingly untenable, even with papal backing. By January of 1215, just three months after his ignominious return from Poitou, the barons were able to force the king to enter negotiations in London.

By this time the baronial demands, which had previously lacked a coherent focus, had been shaped, most acutely by the rediscovery of the Coronation Charter of Henry I. This charter comprised a series of promises, made by Henry I at his Coronation, committing to govern in a fair and just manner, and to limit royal interventions in the affairs of both the barons and the Church. While it is fair to say that the charter was completely ignored by Henry I during much of his reign, the document served as an important precedent, and it was from here that many of the Magna Carta's most genial articles originated, including promises of protection to the widows and children of deceased barons.

The negotiations in London were inconclusive, and King John devoted his subsequent efforts to stalling any future demands, all the while seeking to consolidate the protection afforded him by the papacy. In a particularly desperate move, the king even made the (undoubtedly empty) promise to take up the Cross in crusade, a manoeuvre that won him papal condemnation of the baronial rebellion and perhaps a couple of months' respite. The barons, however, would not be dissuaded, and on 5 May 1215 they renounced their fealty to the king, effectively making a declaration of war.

This was, as the pre-eminent Magna Carta scholar Sir James Holt has suggested, a very curious war, for despite the revocation of fealty neither the barons nor King John seemed inclined towards outright hostilities.[5] Indeed, the barons remained under a guarantee of safe passage for several weeks, and negotiations between the two groups continued with renewed vigour. Safe in the knowledge that Pope Innocent III would find in his favour, King John was quick to suggest that their dispute be arbitrated by a group of eight independent adjudicators, sitting under the direction of the Pope, but remained reticent about committing himself to any genuine concessions.

It wasn't until nearly two weeks after the barons renounced their fealty that the king found his hand forced. On the morning of Sunday 17 May, while most of the city was at Mass, the barons and their associates seized London, and replaced the mayor with one of their own. Unable to wage war against his own capital, King John had no choice but to meet the barons and hear their demands. A truce was hastily arranged, and after much back and forth, the king and the barons assembled on the fields of Runnymede, mid-way between Windsor Castle and the barons' base at Staines.

Exactly how events developed in the days leading up to the sealing of the Magna Carta is poorly documented. We know of at least one draft document – the 'Articles of the Barons' – that seems to have been brought by the barons to form the basis for discussions, but the final charter seems to have been fleshed out over several days of negotiations. Eventually, after what must have been an arduous process, King John set his seal against what was then named only 'The Charter of Runnymede'. The date which heads the Charter is 15 June. By the 19, peace had been declared, London had been returned, and the barons had renewed their pledge of fealty to the king.

Despite appearances, war had not been averted. A mere two months after the charter had been confirmed, the king appealed to the pope, who found the Magna Carta to comprise of promises made under duress, and annulled its content. By September of 1215, the barons had once again renounced their fealty, and declared war on the king. The Magna Carta must have appeared as a dead letter – a mere footnote in the history of English law, alluding only to promises that might have been.

Yet despite its failure in averting civil war, the Magna Carta survived, preserved through a series of reissues made during the reign of King John's son, King Henry III. It was through these reissues that the Magna Carta came to be established in English law, and the Charter of Runnymede came to be known as the Great Charter of the Liberties of England.

> *Despite its failure in averting civil war, the Magna Carta survived, preserved through a series of reissues.*

# the content of the Great Charter

The final version of the original Magna Carta, sealed at Runnymede, is an often confusing mixture of the very specific and the deliberately vague. Split into 63 clauses (with a short preface) by later commentators, it deals largely with the various grievances that the barons had brought against the king.[6] Many of the clauses address the king's financial dealings, placing restrictions on his ability to extract money through inheritance relief (Clauses 2 and 3) and the remarriage of widows (Clause 7), preventing him from unjustly seizing the land of a debtor (Clause 9), and severely limiting the situations in which the king (or any other) could levy tax or scutage without 'the general consent of the realm' (Clauses 12 and 15). There are clauses that deal with the king's ability to make arbitrary demands of his subjects, specifically preventing officers of the king from being able to extract goods or services from free men without their consent (Clauses 28 to 31). Further clauses, meanwhile, deal with the king's exploitation of the judicial system, with regulations placed on the severity of fines (Clauses 20–22), promises made against the arbitrary sale of justice (Clauses 38–40), and a guarantee of regular and accessible court hearings (Clause 18).

While the specifics of the final charter run so far as to determine the exact inheritance relief owed by either a baron or knight (£100 for a baron, £5 for a knight), the charter also embodies certain principles that do not necessarily relate to specific instances. Rather, these act as a framework within which the specific demands can be defined. Three principles are particularly noteworthy.

The first principle is that of 'due process' – emphasising the importance of following legal processes and of operating within a legal framework. Although not referred to directly, allusion to this principle can be found in repeated mentions, in Clauses 21, 39, 52, 56, 57 and 59, of "judgement of peers" as the only legitimate form of judgement. The famous Clause 39 is particularly relevant in this regard, promising that:

> No free man shall be seized or imprisoned, or stripped of his rights or possessions, or outlawed or exiled, or deprived of his standing in any way, nor will we proceed with force against him, or send others to do so, except by the lawful judgment of his peers or by the law of the land.

In demanding that judgement only be passed through the correct legal channels, Clause 39 in many ways reflects the demands of the whole of the Magna Carta, for the claim that underpins the whole rebel enterprise is the claim that justice cannot be held as synonymous with the king's prerogative. Against the arbitrary imposition of fines, levies and punishment, the Magna Carta demands that due process be followed. The judgement of peers was the ultimate embodiment of that principle, because it established the dispensation of justice as something outside of the king's royal control. The law was higher than the king.

The second principle that occurs within the charter is that of arbitration in the king's affairs by a group of twenty-five barons. In Clause 61, the so-called 'security clause', John submits himself, as the monarch, to the judgement of these barons. Should he or one of his officers fail to keep to the promises of liberty made in the Magna Carta, and fail to redress the grievances within forty days once they are raised, then John grants the barons the right to "distrain upon and assail" the king in any way they can. As long as they refrain from causing injury to him or his immediate family, the barons are given permission to seize the king's castles, lands and possessions until amends for the wrong have been made. Furthermore, should the king be accused of unjust gain through fines, or of unjust imprisonment, then Clauses 55 and 52 respectively give this council of barons the authority to settle such disputes through their own judgement. Such statements constituted a radical challenge to the sovereign authority of the monarch.

*Magna Carta might have sprung from narrow self-interests, it sets a precedent in which all free men are privileged certain rights and liberties based on their status as free individuals, rather than on their social worth.*

The third principle of note is the extension of the liberties and rights contained within the charter to those who did not occupy the top strata of English society. Such a move was almost without precedent in the medieval world.[7] Provisions made for "free men" occur in six of the charter's clauses (Clauses 15, 20, 27, 30, 34, 39), and Clause 60 concludes with an exhortation that the liberties in the Magna Carta be extended to all by those in positions of authority. Although it wasn't until the 14th century that "all free men" would be extended to include those in positions of serfdom, and although the rights proclaimed in the 1215 version of the Magna Carta were only ever granted as the concessions of a king, this extension of rights language remains deeply significant. While the Magna Carta might have sprung from narrow self-interests, it sets a precedent in which all free men are privileged certain rights and liberties based on their status as free individuals, rather than on their social worth.

Before all of this, however, right at the beginning of the Magna Carta in the first clause, we have the promise of King John that "the English Church shall be free, and shall have its rights undiminished, and its liberties unimpaired." This promise, and its presence at both the immediate beginning and the very end of the charter, merely hints at the struggle which King John had fought with the English Church in the preceding years of his reign. This was a struggle that would not only have a defining impact on the content and indeed occurrence of the Magna Carta, but that would pave the way for the Magna Carta's affirmation and subsequent immortalization in later reissues. In many ways, the story of the tensions between King John and the English Church is every bit as important to the Magna Carta's legacy as was the conflict with the English barons. However, it is a story that is rarely given the credence it deserves. The next chapter will attempt to rectify that imbalance.

# chapter one – references

1  James Holt, *Magna Carta* (Cambridge: Cambridge University Press, 1992), pp. 151–154.

2  Nicholas Vincent, *Magna Carta: A Very Short Introduction* (Oxford: Oxford University Press, 2012), p. 45.

3  By way of comparison, the 100,000 mark ransom paid by the crown for the safe return of King Richard nearly bankrupted England. 20,000 marks to marry a former queen (who was herself past childbearing age) was an enormous amount of money.

4  See Ralph Turner, *King John: England's Evil King* (Stroud: Tempus, 2005), pp. 87–95.

5  Holt, *Magna Carta*, p. 241.

6  A full translation of the Magna Carta can be found in the appendix of this essay, and all quotations will be referenced with the appropriate clause number.

7  Holt, *Magna Carta*, pp. 277–278.

# the new Becket

## of popes and kings

In order to understand the immediate tensions between King John and the English Church that helped lay the foundations for the Magna Carta, it is necessary first to look back to the reign of Henry I and to the Investiture Controversy of the early 12th century. Prior to the Gregorian reforms of the late 11th century, investiture – the practice of endowing bishops with their titles, lands and authority – had been generally undertaken by the king or emperor, with the approval of the pope or relevant Church authority. This power of investiture endowed the secular rulers of Europe with great influence over Church affairs, for it meant that the monarch could effectively choose who occupied the various bishoprics under their control.

Under Pope Gregory VII, the Church had moved to reassert its authority after a period of instability had seriously weakened papal power – most notably in the claims of a succession of rival antipopes. Key to this reassertion of authority was for the Church to reclaim the power over investiture. For Gregory and his successors, 'lay investiture' (investiture by secular, rather than ecclesial powers) was an undesirable intrusion of royal power into Church matters.

This rejection of lay investiture was problematic for the secular rulers of Europe on a number of levels. First and foremost, it went further than ever before in establishing the papacy and the Church as a separate entity outside of royal control. This was a particularly difficult pill for the Holy Roman Emperor to swallow, as someone who had previously enjoyed an almost sacred status, but in general terms it presented a stark challenge to secular authority across Europe. On a more practical level, the investiture of a new bishop was associated with a number of royally sanctioned privileges – including "endowments, estates and the jurisdictions of his church".[1] The loss of lay investiture could leave royal authority in serious question, and make the monarch obliged to grant privileges to which they would not have otherwise assented.

In England, the particular crisis point arose when Anselm, Archbishop of Canterbury, refused to consecrate those bishops who had been appointed by Henry I during the archbishop's exile. Settlement came in the Concordat of London, confirmed in 1107. Drawing on developments in Church theology that had been focused by the development of canon law, the Concordat made a sharp distinction between the *sacerdotium*, relating to the spiritual realm of the priest, and the *regnum*, relating to the temporal realm of the king. Investiture was defined as a matter of spiritual, rather than temporal authority. The solution put forward therefore saw the king retain control of the distribution of his temporal possessions, meaning that any bishop would still have to pay homage to the king in return for his temporal privileges – his estates and endowments, etc. – but the right to invest individuals with the status and spiritual authority of a bishop or archbishop was to reside solely with the Church.

Despite the compromise reached in the Concordat of London, tensions between Church and state continued to simmer over the course of the 12th century. The culmination of these tensions came in 1170, with the assassination of Thomas Becket, Archbishop of Canterbury during the reign of King Henry II, King John's father and the first of the Plantagenet kings. Becket, previously a close friend of the king, had been a fierce critic of royal interference in Church affairs ever since he first ascended to the archbishopric from his previous role as Chancellor. Particular disagreements had arisen over Henry II's attempts to secure the power to try priests in the royal courts – a power subsequently accorded in the Constitutions of Clarendon – and Becket fled into exile. The Archbishop, deprived of his estates but still retaining his spiritual authority, spent six years in exile on the Continent, from where he excommunicated many of those priests and bishops who supported the king, before returning to Canterbury in June of 1170. In December of that year he was murdered, by knights who apparently felt that they were acting on the guarded instructions of the king himself.

Becket's death was a crucial moment in English history. The assassination was widely regarded as martyrdom, with miracles soon reported at the site of Becket's death, and his canonisation followed quickly, in 1173. Alienated throughout Europe for the murder of a saint, and facing the rebellion of his sons at home, King Henry II was forced to engage in a most remarkable act of public penance at Becket's tomb: submitting himself, topless and on all fours, to flogging from Church prelates and the monks of Canterbury cathedral. With the king quite literally crawling back to the Church, reconciliation with the pope entailed that all previous attempts to secure for the crown a greater authority in ecclesial affairs were abandoned.

*King Henry II may have survived the political crisis surrounding Becket's assassination, but the death left a deep scar on English politics.*

King Henry II may have survived the political crisis surrounding Becket's assassination, but the death left a deep scar on English politics. With the retreat of secular authority from ecclesial affairs, the power of the Church and the papacy was the strongest it had been in centuries. In England particularly, but also on the continent, the newly canonized St Thomas of Canterbury became a figure of legend, and a symbol of anti-monarchical sentiment. It was into such a context that King John would eventually appear, amidst a growing cloud of mistrust and unease surrounding the Plantagenet lineage. His uneasy relationship with the English Church would see the emergence of a 'new Becket', and lay the foundations from which the rebel barons would derive considerable ecclesial support.

> *St Thomas of Canterbury became a figure of legend, and a symbol of anti-monarchical sentiment.*

## the papal interdict

In 1205, six years after John had ascended to the English throne, the incumbent Archbishop of Canterbury, Hubert Walter, died. While John sought to fill the vacant archbishopric with a man of his own choosing – the Bishop of Norwich, John de Gray – the monks of Canterbury Cathedral secretly elected one of their number – the sub-prior Reginald – and dispatched him to Rome for consecration. The eventual arrival in Rome of two competing claimants to the Canterbury See caused Pope Innocent III to reject both claims, and instead ensure the election of a third – the English cardinal and Parisian theologian, Stephen Langton.

Given his status as a man of learning and letters, rather than politics, Langton was a somewhat unusual choice for the role of archbishop. Despite being a prolific writer and highly regarded theologian, he was not well known outside of scholastic circles. The fact that he had spent much of his adult life in Paris, the very city in which King Philip II of France held court, would have done little to endear him to King John, even if he hadn't been thrust upon the English crown.

As it was, Pope Innocent's refusal to consecrate John de Gray did not sit well with King John, who refused to consent to Langton's appointment. The Concordat of London, however, was clear about the division of roles between pope and monarch, and Langton was consecrated, regardless of John's views, at Viterbo in 1207. John responded in kind, refusing to admit Langton to England and driving the Canterbury monks, whom he blamed for the whole affair, into exile. Here, again, was an English monarch demanding the right to be involved in Church affairs.

Innocent's response to John's bullish behaviour was severe. In 1208, England was placed under a papal interdict, and in 1209 King John himself was excommunicated. The interdict meant that the English Church was banned from carrying out its normal duties – the only rites that clergy could perform being the baptism of infants and the absolution of the dying. John demanded that clergy and bishops carry on regardless, stripping any that refused of their estates and privileges. Such punitive measures caused many of the Church's senior clergy to flee the country, and the Church in England was plunged into financial ruin.

As we have already seen, it was John's troubles with the barons that forced him to eventually make amends with the papacy. Admitting Stephen Langton to Canterbury, he promised to repay the Church what had been lost during the interdict, and to restore the lands of exiled clergy. For Archbishop Langton, recovery of the lost revenue and restoration of the Church's estates was a key concern. But as his letters from exile make clear, an even greater concern lay in protecting the Church against future intervention by an English king.[2]

In this mission, Langton had an obvious hero on which to model himself – his own predecessor, Thomas Becket. The Parisian theological school, in which Langton had spent so many years, had long been enamoured with Becket's almost mythological status as a defender of the liberties of the Church against royal intrusion, and Langton's own letters make clear a self-identification with Becket's cause.[3] Neither had the similarities between the two – not least the six years spent in exile at the displeasure of the king – gone unnoticed by others, at a time when the cult of Becket exerted a powerful influence over the English laity.[4] The anonymous 'Song of the Bishops', written in 1208 or 1209, praises Langton not only as "another Thomas (Becket)", but as a prophet in the line of Moses, Phineas and Nathan – prophets sent by God to hold kings to account.[5]

In the short term, Langton had mixed results. An inexperienced political operator, there was little he could do to ensure the king kept up with the promised repayments, particularly once the interdict had been lifted. He also failed to ensure that his own supporters were elected to the vacant bishoprics, with the pope instead favouring those candidates put forward by the king. Yet despite his limitations as a politician, he did have achievements – the most notable of which came in the form of a royal charter, secured in November 1214 and issued again in January 1215, promising free elections for the Church.

## the archbishop as diplomat

Crisis, of course, was just around the corner, and the declaration of war between the king and the barons was a crisis that Langton would inevitably be drawn into. As Archbishop of Canterbury, he had automatically become one of the king's key advisors upon his return to England.[6] Such standing, however, must have put Langton in a difficult position, for while his history with King John and his status as the 'new Becket' no doubt left him with a deep distrust of the king, the pope's unmitigated welcome of King John back into the Christian fold had put pressure on him to publicly endorse the royal position against the barons.

It seems inevitable that Langton would have had some sympathy with the demands of the rebel barons – if not necessarily in terms of the content of their demands, then certainly with the principle that the king should be held to account by a codified system of law. As a scholar in Paris, Langton had used the book of Deuteronomy to expound his belief in the need for a written form of law that would set out the rightful activity of kings, and constrain their habitual excesses.[7] Indeed, Langton's charter of 1214, securing free elections for the Church, would have set a clear and recent precedent for a form of written law that held the king to his promises.

The exact extent to which Langton lent his support to the rebellion is a matter of considerable scholarly debate. Much attention, historically speaking, has been given to the account of Roger of Wendover, the 13th century chronicler, who claims that it was Langton who first introduced the rebel barons to the coronation charter of King Henry I, suggesting it as a basis for their

> *The exact extent to which Langton lent his support to the rebellion is a matter of considerable scholarly debate.*

demands. Later commentators, not least Sir James Holt, have been quick to pour cold water on this idea, labelling Robert an unreliable witness on account of inconsistencies in his narrative.[8] However, as several commentators have pointed out,[9] Langton would certainly have been aware of the coronation charter and would have had access to it in the Canterbury archives. The idea that the Archbishop could have been the avenue by which the barons first started to develop their demands for a charter is certainly a plausible one, even if it cannot be proven.

What is certain is that Langton was heavily involved in the back-and-forth between the two groups, both before and during the negotiations at Runnymede, and that he played a key role in ensuring the barons got a fair hearing from the king. The fact that he is named, in Clause 55, as a key arbiter in future disputes, shows how intimately he was associated with the baronial cause. The historian Maurice Powicke suggests that it was Langton who first encouraged the king to offer the barons concessions, in the form of a council of arbitration.[10] His privileged position – as a man invested with spiritual authority directly from the pope, rather than the king – would have meant he was one of the few men in England able to show some sympathy with the rebel cause without fear of the king's reprisals. The ghost of Becket loomed large, and King John could ill-afford any disruption to his newly established relationship with Rome.

The extent of Langton's sympathy for the rebel cause is perhaps best illustrated by events that occurred after the failure of the Magna Carta, three months after it had been sealed. In his annulment of the promises made in the charter, the pope had demanded the excommunication of those barons who had made such demands of the king. Langton, however, refused. What papal support he still retained was at this point lost, and King John, who had long grown suspicious of Langton's loyalties, was once again able to send him into exile – this time with the full support of the papacy.

We should not imagine that Langton's sympathy with the rebel demands would have persuaded him to throw his lot completely in with the rebel camp. He was a deeply conservative character, for whom divine authority was granted to kings and rulers in St Paul's letter to the Romans, chapter 13.[11] There is no suggestion in the records that he actively joined the rebels, or ever came close to renouncing his fealty to the king. But the fact that he did provide tacit support for the rebel barons serves to illustrate just how intimately the Church was involved in shaping events that led to the Magna Carta. It was not just Langton, either, who provided the rebel barons with ecclesial backing. Indeed, many bishops and theologians were far more vocal than the Archbishop in promoting the rebel cause. These rebel clergy included the Archbishop of Canterbury's own brother (and candidate for the Archbishopric of York), Simon Langton, and the Bishop of Hereford, Giles de Briouze – one of the key leaders of the baronial revolt. The canon and later chancellor of St Paul's, Gervase of Howbridge, and the archbishop's steward, Elias of Dereham, were also vocal supporters of the barons and the aims of the Magna Carta. If Langton never offered the barons the direct support of the Church, it is highly significant that many of those in his most intimate circle did.[12]

## the archbishop as author

*At the beginning of the 20th century, Langton was widely assumed to be the principal author of the Magna Carta.*

Given his background as a scholar, his popular status as the new Becket, and his prominent role in the negotiations, it is perhaps unsurprising that, at the beginning of the 20th century, Langton was widely assumed to be the principal author of the Magna Carta. Such a belief was, however, based more on popular perceptions of the Archbishop and on the suspect accounts of Roger of Wendover, than on any detailed historical study, and it has been treated with a great deal more scepticism in the last century. Certainly it seems highly unlikely that Langton was involved to any great extent in actually writing the Articles of the Barons, which the rebels brought to Runnymede to form the basis of negotiations.[13] And while there are a number of features in the Magna Carta's final form that would certainly have sat well with Langton's theological inclinations, it is too great a leap to attribute them solely or directly to him. As has been pointed out by other commentators, short of discovering a version of the Magna Carta with Langton's contributions highlighted and singled out, we will never truly know exactly who wrote what.[14]

Having said that, there is one key aspect of the Magna Carta in which Langton's hand is clear. This is the first clause, guaranteeing the English Church her traditional rights and liberties, including freedom of elections. Langton had already secured such guarantees in the charter of 1214, but here we have a further confirmation of the right of the Church to operate free of royal interference. Given that the clause harkens back to the previous charter, confirmed by the king "before the outbreak of the present dispute between us and our barons", and given that no such clause appears in the Articles of the Barons, the insertion of this opening clause must surely have come directly from Langton.

The significance of the appearance of this clause, inserted by Langton right at the beginning of the Magna Carta, is easy to miss. The way that the preamble, outlining the hereditary titles of the king, and listing those counsellors in attendance, flows so neatly into a confirmation of the status of the English Church (and the fact that this confirmation of status is so clearly distinct from the concessions that follow), leaves the casual reader with the impression that reference to the liberties of the Church is all a matter of ceremony, with the real concessions listed afterwards. The fact, too, that this is a *confirmation* of the liberties of the Church, rather than anything new or original, gives credence to the notion that Clause 1 is of no great importance. As Professor of Medieval History David Carpenter puts it,

> we are so used to the clause being there, that we just take it for granted. Historians thus usually ascribe it to Langton in perfunctory fashion, before moving on to other more exciting things, as though the inclusion of the church was as routine as it was insignificant.[15]

There was, of course, good reason on Langton's part to ensure that the content of the first clause was kept separate from the concessions that followed. The fact that the king had already granted free elections to the Church meant such a concession could stand independently of the success or failure of the Magna Carta – something that Clause 1 emphasises through its reminder that King John had already granted such concessions of his own free will, and under no duress. Langton must have known the Magna Carta, sealed by the king under the threat of civil war, would be open to repeal by the pope, despite the assurances that the barons extracted. If the Magna Carta was defeated, the Archbishop did not want the principle of ecclesial liberty going down with it.

This fact invites the question of why Langton felt compelled to tie ecclesial liberty to the future of the Magna Carta at all. In part, it must have been a calculated gamble – should the Magna Carta survive and become law, then the independence of the Church would have been secured in perpetuity, in a form that would supersede the concessions already granted in the 1214 charter.[16] That a version of this clause (from the 1225 issue of the Magna Carta) remains on the statute books to this day, is a testament to Langton's foresight and ingenuity. However, there is also a sense that such an important document as the Magna Carta would have been felt to be lacking had it neglected to mention the Church. By placing the principle of ecclesial liberty first and foremost in the Magna Carta, just as Henry I had done in his coronation charter, Langton reinforced the existing notion that a right relationship with the Church – respect for her traditional rights and liberties and so on – was a necessary precondition for any right relationship between the king and the wider community.[17]

Whatever the reasons, the fact that Langton tied ecclesial liberty so closely to the Magna Carta is of enormous significance, for the inclusion of this clause gave the Church, and not least the bishops, a major stake in the Magna Carta's survival. The inclusion meant that the Magna Carta was not only destined to become a symbol to the English bishops of the limits of monarchical sovereignty,[18] but to become more specifically a symbol for the liberty and freedom of the Church from royal intrusion.[19] From the outset, it was bishops who played a vital role in distributing copies of the Charter in the local parishes.[20] Far more importantly, however, it was senior bishops and archbishops who were instrumental in securing the Magna Carta's numerous reissues during the reign of King Henry III.

> Because of Langton's innovation, the Church would go on to throw its considerable weight behind the Great Charter.

Returning from exile in 1218, Archbishop Langton was particularly influential in securing the 1225 reissue – the first version to be issued "spontaneously, and of [the king's] own free will", thereby removing all traces of coercion that had characterised previous versions. Such was the strength of Langton's backing, that he issued the 1225 version with a sentence of excommunication against any king, officer or baron who broke the Charter's laws. It was this 1225 version that would go on to become a central part of English law, and would eventually form the foundation upon which the language of rights and liberties (in the modern sense) could be built. Had the Church not been committed to the principles of ecclesial liberty contained within the text, there is no way of knowing whether such reissues would have been achieved.

King John's struggle with the English Church then, and the subsequent inclusion of the language of ecclesial liberty within the text of the Magna Carta, was to prove decisive, for the complex dynamic between the Church and the king gave ecclesial authorities a vested interest in any attempt to limit the monarch's ability to interfere in Church affairs. Because of Langton's innovation, the Church would go on to throw its considerable weight behind the Great Charter. Without that crucial contribution, there is a very real possibility that 2015 would mark the 800th anniversary of nothing more than a failed rebellion.

# chapter two – references

1   Colin Morris, *The Papal Monarchy: The Western Church from 1050 to 1250* (Oxford: Oxford University Press, 1991), p. 156.

2   Nicholas Vincent, "Stephen Langton, Archbishop of Canterbury" in *Etienne Langton: prédicateur, bibliste, théologien*, ed. L-J Bataillon, N. Beriou, G. Dahan and R. Quinto (Turnhout 2010), pp. 69–70.

3   See ibid, pp. 68–70.

4   Langton had even chosen to spend his exile in the very Abbey where Becket had sought refuge from King Henry II between 1165 and 1166.

5   Ibid, p. 86.

6   See Maurice Powicke, *Stephen Langton*, (Oxford: Oxford University Press, 1928), pp. 106–9.

7   John Baldwin, "Master Stephen Langton, Future Archbishop of Canterbury: The Paris Schools and the Magna Carta" in *English Historical Review*, Vol. 123, No. 503 (Oxford: Oxford University Press, 2008), 813, and David D'Avray, "Magna Carta: its background in Stephan Langton's academic Biblical Exegesis and its Episcopal Reception" in *Studi Medievali* (1997), p. 429.

8   Holt, Magna Carta, pp. 224–226.

9   See particularly Vincent, "Stephen Langton", p. 93.

10  Powicke, *Stephen Langton*, p. 125.

11  Baldwin, "Master Stephen Langton", p. 819.

12  Holt, *Magna Carta*, p. 283.

13  See David Carpenter's persuasive account of why Langton could not have been the author of the Articles – David Carpenter, "Archbishop Langton and Magna Carta: His Contribution, His Doubts and His Hypocrisy" in *English Historical Review*, Vol. 126, No. 522 (Oxford: Oxford University Press, 2011), pp. 1044–1047.

14  Vincent, "Stephen Langton", p. 97.

15  Carpenter, "Archbishop Langton", p. 1050.

16  Ibid, p. 1054.

17  Nederman, "The Liberty of the Church", p. 459.

18  D'Avray, "Magna Carta", p. 432.

19  Carpenter, "Archbishop Langton", p. 1057.

20  Ibid, p. 1056.

# the theological roots of liberty and right

## the theological framework of the Magna Carta

We have seen how the relationship between the king and the church played a vital role in the development and preservation of the Magna Carta. However, it would be a mistake to think that the Christian Church's contribution to this period in English history is limited to practical or reactionary politics. There is, as was alluded to in the introduction to this essay, a bigger story at play here – a story about the development of ideas, in which the Magna Carta can be seen as the first cogent political expression of certain theories of right and liberty. This story is one in which the Christian Church and Christian theology plays a vital role.

The purpose of this chapter is to look at that wider story in more detail: to look at the context – specifically the theological context – within which certain ideas contained in the Magna Carta arose. In chapter one, we identified three principles that provide the framework for many of the Magna Carta's specific demands: the importance of following to due legal process, the legitimacy of baronial arbitration in the king's affairs, and the extension of rights language to "all free men". What this third and final chapter will attempt to show is that these ideas, novel and original though they were, did not arise out of thin air. They were ideas borne of a developing intellectual tradition that was itself rooted in Christian thought.

Such a suggestion encounters an immediate difficulty, for the extent to which contemporary scholarship has drawn a positive link between the theological ideas of the early 13th century and the formulation of the Magna Carta is relatively limited. This fact stems from two problems. The first problem is the relative lack of theological literacy among historians of political theory. Despite the intimate connection between theology and politics, particularly in the medieval period, the history of political thought and the history of theological thought have largely developed as separate disciplines in separate university faculties. Where that gap has been bridged, it has usually been done by experts in ecclesiastical history, rather than those who specialise in systematic theology. Thus, where discussion of the Church's role in the Magna Carta has taken place, it has usually been framed by a discussion about practical Church politics – the tensions between Church and state highlighted in the previous chapter for example – rather than a discussion about theological ideas. Experts versed in theological *and* political thought are a rare breed indeed, and academic discussion of the ideas underpinning the Magna Carta has reflected this fact.

The second problem that has led to a limited academic focus on the role of theology in laying the ideological foundations for the Magna Carta, is the difficulty inherent in tracing the development of an idea from ideological principle to political practice. It is, of course, relatively easy to trace the development of a practical need or desire into a practical solution. We can clearly see how the practical self-interest of the barons and the bishops – the desire for greater control over their own affairs, for example – led them to place practical safeguards within the Magna Carta that would prevent infringements by the king. However, it is more difficult to track how the individuals who wrote the Magna Carta might have been influenced by more speculative ideals, or to say exactly how certain theological precepts came to be enshrined within its clauses. It is much easier to focus on the material and practical demands of the day than to think more speculatively about the influence of ideas and theology.

These difficulties should not leave us thinking that an enquiry into the theological context of the Magna Carta is a fruitless exercise, however. We may be entering relatively uncharted waters, but they can still be richly rewarding. By looking more generally at the theological and philosophical climate in which the Great Charter was written, we will be in a better position to understand the roots from which the principles that framed the Magna Carta grew. And it is worth bearing in mind that, according to Barack Obama at least, the principles that framed the Magna Carta form the foundations from which we derive our modern understandings of human liberty and right.

Before we move on to look at these principles in detail, however, it is necessary to say a few words about one of the most important developments in medieval theology to have emerged over the course of the 12th and early 13th centuries. This was the formation and continued development of a theologically reflective and coherent canon law. A central moment in this development was the completion of the *Decretum* of the medieval canonist Gratian, otherwise known as the *Condordance of Discordant Canons*, in the middle of the 12th century. The *Decretum* was an enormous work, bringing together sources from various papal decrees, Church councils, the Bible, the Church Fathers, and bits of Roman law. It was intended as a complete compendium of canon law, and was quickly accepted as authoritative. The task that Gratian had set himself was to establish a framework in which these 'discordant canons' – often contrasting and opposed – could be reconciled in a single coherent system. Its influence was widespread, inspiring hundreds of commentaries (the writings of the so-called 'Decretists'), many of which constituted great works of theology in their own right. As Brian Tierney puts it, "the work of these Decretists, most of them unpublished so far, contain the most sophisticated thought of the age on problems of church and state".[1] As we shall see, the development of canon law, and particularly of the *Decretum*, contributed greatly to the systematisation and renewal of theological thought throughout the 12th and 13th centuries.

# the importance of due legal process

In chapter one, we saw that the principle of due process that underpins the Magna Carta was best demonstrated through repeated demands for the "judgement of peers". That the Magna Carta assumes judgement by peers to be the only legitimate form of judgement should not surprise us, nor should we think that such an assumption was a radical or revolutionary one. Trial by ordeal – the main alternative to peer judgement – had been in long decline in the Western world, particularly in England since the legal reforms of King Henry II. This decline had been hastened by theological concerns about the legitimacy of 'tempting God' to perform a miraculous judgement, and concerns that priests involved in 'blood punishments' were corrupted by association. Only five months after the events at Runnymede, the Fourth Lateran Council forbade priests from blessing the ordeals. Given that the ordeal required a priestly blessing to ensure God's righteous judgement, this ban served as an effective ban on the ordeal itself.

While we should not be surprised that the Magna Carta regards the judgement of peers as the only legitimate form of judgement, neither should we imagine that its focus on peer judgement as a central aspect of a proper legal process is unimportant. The slow death of trial by ordeal throughout the 12th century, and the focus on peer judgement that accompanied it, yielded a growth of theological thought that had a profound impact on the intellectual foundations of the Magna Carta. As we shall see, the theological movement from divine judgement to human judgement, of which the demise of trial by ordeal is a crucial part, laid many of the foundations from which the barons could demand a proper and binding legal process.

In his book, *The Origins of Reasonable Doubt*, James Whitman, Law Professor at Yale Law School, argues that the ultimate concern of the medieval judiciary was not necessarily how to identify factual proof, but how to absolve oneself of moral responsibility for the outcome of judgement.[2] This was an issue that had existed ever since Christianity had become adopted as the religion of the Roman Empire – and Christians had found themselves in positions of authority, required to dispense justice.

The great concern of the Christian legal system, since the time of Augustine, had been that in condemning people to death, judges effectively became responsible for murder in the eyes of God – particularly if they inadvertently condemned an innocent party. The trial by ordeal had developed as a way of leaving judgement – and therefore responsibility for judgement – in the hands of the divine, of "shifting the odium of human responsibility to God", as Whitman puts it.[3] The decline of the ordeal in the 11th and 12th centuries thus threatened to implicate those who administered justice in the guilt of mortal sin.

The solution to this problem required the development of a delicate theological framework that sought to absolve judges of moral responsibility in cases of blood punishment. This framework drew heavily on the theology of the Church Fathers St Jerome and St Augustine, who had been faced with very similar problems in their own time. Augustine's resolution, that "when a man is killed justly, it is the law that kills him, not [the judge]" was a formulation that entered into canon law through Gratian's *Decretum*,[4] from where it had a marked effect on theological thinking. The conclusion arose that anyone condemned to death in accordance with the law of the land was condemned by the law itself, rather than the judge who administered it. Guilt only arose when a judge failed to pass judgement according to the precepts of the law. Thus, the canonist Raymond of Penafort wrote, at the beginning of the 13th century:

> If it is done out of love of justice, the judge does not sin in condemning [the accused] to death and ordering his minister to kill him, nor is the minister condemned if he kills having been ordered to do so. Still, either of them will commit mortal sin if he does it without observing the procedures of the law.[5]

The medieval focus on a due and proper legal process develops, therefore, out of a theological concern for the guilt of those charged with the dispensation of justice. It was only by establishing 'the procedures of the law', that those who sat in positions of judgement could be absolved of moral responsibility for their judicial decisions. In so far as the judiciary followed a developed legal process, it was the law that shouldered the burden of responsibility for punishing the guilty party.

This concept of due process pervades the Magna Carta, not simply in its appeals to "the lawful judgement of peers and the law of the land", but in the fact that the basic purpose of the charter was to set out what constitutes right and proper action on the part of the governing authority. With this in mind, it is particularly relevant that this question of due process within a legal framework was a major theological concern of none other than Archbishop Stephen Langton. The historian John Baldwin, in his meticulous study of the Paris school in which Langton studied and taught, highlights several key works in which Langton explores the theme of due process and its implications for political legitimacy.[6] The most important of these for our present discussion is a series of *questionnes* relating to the circumstances in which resistance to temporal authority can be theologically sanctioned.

As previously noted, Langton was a deeply conservative character, for whom the authority endowed on the temporal rulers of this world in Paul's Epistle to the Romans should be taken with the utmost seriousness. But it remained a topic of much debate among even the most conservative theologians as to how far Christians should be "subject to the governing authorities". Clearly a temporal ruler could not compel a Christian to renounce their allegiance to Christ. How far then, should Christians obey a ruler who commanded that which ran contrary to the will of God in other areas of the political life?

Langton's theological work addresses two particular examples – examples that had also been closely linked in the thought of Augustine. The first example asks how a Christian should respond to someone unjustly condemned to die by the king, while the second asks how a Christian should respond to an unjust declaration of war by the king. Like Augustine, Langton provides the same response for both situations. The king should be obeyed, even by a Christian charged with the execution of an innocent party, but *only as long as the king's sentence has been passed by a legitimate court.*

> If the matter was judged through a sentence by a court, even though the court was partial to the prince, and even though the sentence was unjust, the people must accept, obey and not discuss the sentence… Disobedience is permitted only when the matter has not been adjudicated.[7]

When we read such comments in the light of our previous discussion about the theological problems associated with human judgement, it becomes clear that Langton's regard for the due process of law is borne out of theological, as opposed to simply practical, concerns. The demand for a process of law, just like the demand for judgement by peers, is borne from a concern to protect those in authority from moral responsibility in their decision making. Just as the judicial process protected judges from the guilt associated with capital punishment and miscarriages of justice, so legal process protected the king from the guilt associated with waging war and condemning individuals to death – even when done unjustly. In so far as they follow the processes and precepts of the law, temporal rulers are able to put forth judgements without accusations of mortal sin. It is the law that shoulders the burden of responsibility for the execution of unjust action, rather than the king.

*The medieval focus on a due and proper legal process develops, therefore, out of a theological concern for the guilt of those charged with the dispensation of justice.*

In many ways, such a move would have been designed to protect the sovereignty of the king from being called into question. Just like the medieval desire to absolve judges of mortal sin, so Langton was presumably concerned with the spiritual position of the king. A king whose judgements left him open to the possibility of mortal sin posed a serious theological problem for someone committed to the authority of the monarch as laid down in Paul's Epistle to the Romans. Thus there was a need to protect the monarch from such responsibility. However, Langton's resolution also had the very real effect of placing the authority of the king *under* the authority of the law, rather than above it. We have already seen that Langton finds scriptural precedent for such a move in the book of Deuteronomy, as an example of written law intended to serve as a framework in which kingly authority could operate.[8] Pierre de Chanter, Langton's mentor (and incidentally a key figure in the attack on trial by ordeal), had written in a similar vein about a passage from the Biblical Book of Samuel, in which the prophet inscribes the law of the land in a book, to mark the coronation of King Saul.[9] He, like Langton, claimed that this example demonstrated biblical precedent for a law that stated the limits of what kings could demand from their subjects.[10]

It was suggested at the beginning of this chapter that trying to identify how certain theological precepts and ideas came to lay the foundations of the Magna Carta might be a step too far. Here, however, we might have an exception, for Langton's close association with the principle of due process makes him an ideal candidate for the transmission of such ideas. It is also highly relevant that, in one of his more colourful stories, Roger of Wendover tells a tale in which the recently-returned Archbishop chastises King John for resolving to make war without a judgement from his court.[11] Whether or not this story is true is largely irrelevant. What it shows is how intimately Langton was associated with the principle of due process and the legitimacy granted by a court of law – not just in his theological writings at Paris, but in the popular imagination of 13th century England.

Whether or not it entered the Magna Carta through Langton, the principle of due process is an essential feature of medieval developments in legal and political thought. In so far as it places the authority of law above that of the king, the Magna Carta can thus be seen as a central development in the movement from a feudal, hierarchical vision of sovereignty, in which the king is the source of all temporal authority (an authority which is itself derived from God), to a contractual vision of sovereignty, in which the king or ruling body is subject to the law and answerable to its precepts. What has not always been recognised is that this principle of due process is one deeply influenced by the precepts of medieval theology. A theological concern for the moral guilt of those in positions of judgement and authority led to a heightened regard for legal process in the medieval mind. In so far as those in authority followed the procedures of the law, then it was the law that killed, and not the judge or king.

# the legitimacy of action taken against the king

The Magna Carta did not simply decree that the king should follow the precepts of law. It also decreed that he should be held to account, should he fail to keep to the promises of the charter. This was the rationale behind the so-called 'security clause' of Clause 61, in which the king granted a council of twenty-five barons the right to hold him and his descendants to account, through force of arms if necessary.

> *The Magna Carta did not simply decree that the king should follow the precepts of law. It also decreed that he should be held to account, should he fail to keep to the promises of the charter.*

Clause 61 did not survive as part of the Magna Carta after 1215. The all-important reissue of 1225, during the reign of King Henry III, had no such security mechanism in place to ensure that the king kept to the promises of the charter. It wasn't until the 17th century and the absolutist claims of Charles I that the 61st clause of the original Magna Carta was rediscovered and celebrated as protection against royal tyranny. The clause never entered law, and the council of twenty-five barons was never successfully convened.

This does not mean, however, that the presence of the security clause in the 1215 issue of the Magna Carta is at all insignificant. In the history of Western law, it is one of the earliest (if not the very first) examples of a legal framework which held the monarchy to account for the fulfilment of their promises.[12] It might not have been a particularly realistic system, or at all successful, but in so far as it facilitated legally sanctioned resistance to an unjust or tyrannical king, the inclusion of Clause 61 in the Magna Carta is a deeply symbolic moment in the evolution of Western thought. It is a moment that was preceded and informed by developments in a number of areas, but key among these was developments in theological thinking about the legitimacy of authority. Here, as in the demand for due process, the Church played a key role in laying the intellectual foundations for the Magna Carta's specific demands.

The crucial text in this regard emerged in the mid-12th century: the *Policraticus*, written by Paris-educated theologian and secretary to the Archbishop of Canterbury, John of Salisbury. This enormous and wide-ranging treatise is widely regarded as the first complete work of western political theory to be produced since the time of Augustine, bringing much of the theological and philosophical thought of the Latin Middle Ages to bear on issues of political theory. Most controversially, and most significantly for us, the *Policraticus* contains a number of highly influential reflections on what can and should be done about tyrannical rulers.

Book IV of the *Policraticus* constitutes an extended discussion of what John of Salisbury considers to be the nature of a prince (by which he means any righteous ruler or monarch), and of what separates the prince from the tyrant.[13] In this regard, the *Policraticus* draws heavily on the theme of due legal process that we have just discussed. Absolutely central to the role of the prince is the principle of law, and the need for rulers to follow due process in the execution of legal judgements.[14] The prince is distinguished from the tyrant, according to John, by his obedience to the law, and by his willingness to submit himself to its authority.[15] While temporal authority is something ordained by God, this does not mean the prince can act with impunity.

> *In so far as it facilitated legally sanctioned resistance to an unjust or tyrannical king, the inclusion of Clause 61 in the Magna Carta is a deeply symbolic moment in the evolution of Western thought.*

The *Policraticus*, however, goes much further than identifying how a temporal ruler *should* behave. That in itself would not have been particularly unusual. Where the *Policraticus* goes further, and where it is most revolutionary, is its allusion to what John believes should happen to a tyrant – a temporal ruler who refuses to submit themselves to the law.

> It is not only permitted, but it is also equitable and just to slay tyrants. For he who receives the sword deserves to perish by the sword. But 'receives' is to be understood to pertain to he who has rashly usurped that which is not his, not to he who receives what he uses from the power of God. He who receives power from God serves the laws and is the slave of justice and right. He who usurps power supresses justice and places the laws beneath his will.[16]

This apparent demand, that members of the public take arms against tyrannical rulers, can be difficult to reconcile within the rest of John's work. John of Salisbury, like Stephen Langton after him, was a theologian who held the authority of rulers in the highest regard, rooted as it was in Paul's Epistle to the Romans. His argument elsewhere in the *Policraticus,* that "all power is from the Lord God" and that "whoever resists power, resists what is ordained by God",[17] makes it difficult to see how he can then advocate the killing of those in positions of authority.

We can find an allusion to the reconciliation of this view on tyranny, however, in the very language of prince and tyrant that the *Policraticus* uses. When a prince submits himself to the law, he does so because his will is in accordance with the will and justice of God. Thus, John suggests that we can't even speak of the will of the prince "since in such matters he is not permitted his own will unless it is permitted by law or equity, or brings about judgements for the common utility".[18] Being a "true" prince is *defined* by having a will that is in accord with the will of God. The will of the tyrant, on the other hand, is shaped by his own arbitrary desire. The implication is that a tyrant, in so far as he fails to exhibit the central characteristic of a "true" prince, is no prince at all. He is, in the language John uses, a "usurper" – an illegitimate ruler to whom the language of authority and subsequent demand for obedience found in Paul's Epistle to the Romans does not apply.

This position is a deeply theological one, rooted in the belief that secular laws are not simply arbitrary standards and impositions, but reflected the amalgamation of divinely ordained natural law and human custom – a position that had itself been borne out in Gratian's *Decretum*. A ruler who eschewed the law – and with it the natural law and justice of God – was no ruler at all.

This position is one that would go on to become deeply ingrained within Western theological and political discourse. One of the most controversial debates to emerge out of the development of canon law in the latter half of the 12th century, was what the Church would be able to do were it to be confronted by a heretical or overly-licentious pope. Such a suggestion was certainly not unfounded – the *Decretum* had made reference to several historical popes of dubious moral and theological character, and medieval Christianity was well aware that the man who assumed the Chair of St Peter retained his fallible human nature.

One of the most influential responses to this problem came from the medieval canonist Huguccio, possibly the greatest of the many medieval commentators on Gratian's *Decretum*. Huguccio's highly influential solution to the problem of a heretical pope was to argue that a pope who adhered to heretical views, or persisted in a notorious sin after due admonition, simply ceased to be pope at all. The very phrase 'heretical pope' was, for Huguccio, a contradiction in terms, and any pope who thus contradicted the very foundations of their papacy could be removed by the Church without any injury to the Papal See. This ingenious solution, as the historian Brian Tierney rightly points out, defended both the welfare of the Church against a corrupting papacy, and the integrity of papal sovereignty.[19]

The Magna Carta, of course, does not employ the language of prince and tyrant. It doesn't question the king's right to rule. All the laws of the Magna Carta, including the security measures of Clause 61, are framed as the concessions of a king, rather than as the natural rights of the populace. But it is not hard to see the links between the intellectual climate outlined above and the political reality of the Magna Carta. The intellectual and theological context of the early 13th century would have been fertile ground for the legitimation of direct action against a king who had failed to uphold due process and the laws of the land. Furthermore, the association that John of Salisbury drew between the divinely-ordained authority of the king and the king's regard for the will and justice of God as expressed in law, is an association to which the Magna Carta directly alludes in the way it structures the security clause.

> If we… make no redress [of the offence against the Magna Carta]… the four barons shall refer the matter to the rest of the twenty-five barons, who may distrain upon and assail us in every way possible, with the support of the whole community of the land… until they have secured such redress as they have determined upon. Having secured the redress, they are to resume their normal obedience to us.

*The Magna Carta draws a direct link between the king's duty to follow the law of the Magna Carta, and the duty of the king's subjects to pay fealty to their monarch.*

Here, the Magna Carta draws a direct link between the king's duty to follow the law of the Magna Carta, and the duty of the king's subjects to pay fealty to their monarch. If the king neglects his duty to the people, then the people are absolved from their own duty to the king, until they have brought him back into line. As would be expected of a royal charter, the Magna Carta demands that the overall intention of any action taken against the king be to bring him back to the justice of God, rather than remove him from power. But this does not negate the fact that the Magna Carta allows (or even demands) the temporary revocation of fealty to a king who persistently disregards its laws.

Very few scholars have attempted to make direct links between 12th century political thought regarding legitimate authority and the content of the Magna Carta. The German scholar of medieval history Natalie Fryde is one of the few to make a direct link to John of Salisbury – suggesting Archbishop Langton as the avenue for the transmission of the idea that rebellion to tyranny was legitimated by the tyrants disregard for the law and due process.[20] This may be overstating the case for Langton, whose natural conservatism would presumably have made him nervous of the suggestion of outright rebellion against a king. Langton, after all, doesn't seem to have made quite the same link between the legitimacy of a ruler and their regard for the divine will that John of Salisbury had made. In Langton's framework, an unjust king retains authority, so long as he operates through a legitimate court. However, whether or not Langton acted as a vehicle of transmission is rather irrelevant. The works of John of Salisbury and Huguccio were widely read and their ideas widely disseminated by the early 13th century. There are plenty of other avenues by which these deeply theological ideas could have percolated through to the Magna Carta.

# the extension of rights to 'all free men'

The third and final principle that we noted as providing a framework for the Magna Carta's specific demands is the extension of the rights contained within the Magna Carta to "all free men" of England, as demonstrated in Clause 60:

> All these customs and liberties that we have granted shall be observed in our kingdom in so far as concerns our own relations with our subjects. Let all men of our kingdom, whether clergy or laymen, observe them similarly in their relations with their own men.

This extension of rights is not a simple afterthought, however, expressed in this single clause at the end of the Charter. It is something that frames the whole of the Magna Carta, appearing right at the beginning in the first clause ("to all free men of our kingdom we have also granted, for us and our heirs for ever, all the liberties written out below") and throughout the intervening clauses. Clause 27, for example, states that "If a free man dies intestate, his movable goods are to be distributed by his next-of-kin and friends", while Clause 30 guarantees that "no sheriff, royal official, or other person shall take horses or carts for transport from any free man, without his consent". Clause 39, of course, contains the famous promise that "no free man shall be seized or imprisoned... except by the lawful judgement of his peers".

It is important to understand what sort of rights we are here dealing with. There is an obvious temptation to attribute to Magna Carta some sort of expression of inalienable, fundamental or inherent human rights, particularly given its association with the formation of the United States Declaration of Independence. Yet, as numerous commentators have pointed out, this temptation would be erroneous. The Magna Carta is "no blanket or universal statement of civic or inherent right".[21] It is a body of *acquired* rights, granted in the form of a royal concession.

It is also important to understand to whom the Magna Carta was directed when it referred to "all free men". The majority of peasants under the English feudal system were serfs (referred to as 'villeins' in the Articles of the Barons and in the Magna Carta) – men and women who were bound (either through promise or inheritance) to a particular plot of land, owned by a particular lord. Although not technically slaves, neither were they free. The Magna Carta, then, has very little to say about this lowest stratum of English society – another reason why we should not see the rights it conveys as somehow inherent to human nature.

Nevertheless, this extension of rights language to all minor landowners and tenants was highly unusual in the early 13th century and unparalleled in contemporary charters and statutes across Europe. At a time when legislation was traditionally concerned with the protection of the rights of elites, the Magna Carta "assumed legal parity among all free men to an exceptional degree".[22] Its specific clauses might have been predominantly shaped by the self-interested motives of the barons, but its scope extended well beyond these narrow confines. Although generally restricted to "all free men", the charter even went so far as to create provision for serfs in Clause 20, in which it promises that a villein will not be denied "the implements of his husbandry, if they fall upon the mercy of a royal court". The final version of the Magna Carta, then, was not a charter for the privileged few, but a charter for the whole community of England, even if that community inevitably and to differing extents excluded serfs, vagrants, women, and children.

> The final version of the Magna Carta, then, was not a charter for the privileged few, but a charter for the whole community of England, even if that community inevitably and to differing extents excluded serfs, vagrants, women, and children.

Given this radical extension of the language of rights, it is highly significant that the language and understanding of rights underwent significant development in the latter half of the 12th century, particularly within the Church. Yet again, this shift had been greatly influenced by the development of canon law, and especially by Gratian's *Decretum*. In his attempt to reconcile the Church's discordant canons, Gratian had established certain principles as the key to discerning the proper interpretation of canon law. The most important of these principles he lays out right at the beginning of the work:

> The human race is ruled by a twofold rule, namely, natural law and practices. Natural law is that which is contained in the law and the Gospel, by which each person is commanded to do to others what he would wish to be done to himself, and forbidden to render to others that which he would not have done to himself. Hence, Christ says in the Gospel, 'All things whatever that you would wish other people to do to you, do the same also to them. For this is the law and the prophets.'[23]

In Gratian's understanding, the so-called 'golden rule' lies at the very heart of justice – and should thus lie at the very heart of earthly laws. This might sound unsurprising to the modern ear, but in the 12th century it would have been something of revelation. As the Political Philosopher Larry Siedentop suggests:

> By identifying natural law with biblical revelation and Christian morality, Gratian gave it an egalitarian basis – and a subversive potential – utterly foreign to the ancient world's understanding of natural law as 'everything in its place'[24]

The "subversive potential" of such a revisionist approach to the concept of natural law lay in the fact that Gratian's *Decretum* treated all persons as equal before the natural law of God. The natural law as conceived by Gratian refused to differentiate between persons based on their status, for the golden rule commands that everyone do to others as they would have done to themselves. If all persons stood equally before natural law however, and if natural law formed the basis of human law, then the unavoidable implication was that all persons should also stand equal before human law.

This egalitarian line of thinking would go on to mark a subtle shift in the way that medieval Europe thought about whom the law was intended to serve. Rather than serve the king or the state in the preservation of the "natural" social order, the law came to be seen as an instrument of justice intended to serve the whole populace. Thus Pope Innocent III, writing in 1204, would declare:

> It may be said that kings are to be treated differently from others. We, however, know that it is written in the divine law, 'You shall judge the great as well as the little and there shall be no difference of persons'.[25]

A number of eminent scholars have identified this shift as the root from which we have come to speak of natural or inherent human rights.[26] The statement that all humans are fundamentally equal before God naturally lent itself to the suggestion that humans have a 'natural' responsibility towards each other. This was particularly true with regards to the poor, for the *Decretum* contained a number of striking warnings that suggested a failure to feed the poor left the wealthy responsible for their deaths (e.g. "Feed the poor. If you do not feed them you kill them," and "A man who keeps more for himself than he needs is guilty of theft").[27] The question that subsequently arose was whether the poor had a *right* to claim subsistence from the wealthy in times of need.[28] Such a line of thinking was one that was as deeply indebted to the Scriptures and to the Early Church Fathers, as it was to Gratian.[29] A fundamentally egalitarian message was central to the Christian gospel, and the development of a coherent framework of canon law had allowed this fact to once more to thrust itself into the public sphere.

How far we understand the significance of this development of an egalitarian understanding of the purpose law to the development of the Magna Carta depends on how far we imagine the Magna Carta's extension of rights language to "all free men" to have an egalitarian basis. While Gratian's egalitarian basis for natural law found in the *Decretum* might have laid the foundation for future language about inalienable or intrinsic human rights, this is not the form of 'rights' that what we find in the Magna Carta. Neither did the Magna Carta go so far as to proclaim all men fundamentally or intrinsically equal, for it still assumed the basic structure of a feudal hierarchy. Yet the extension of rights language to those from the lower strata of society was a radical and significant one. In so far as it entered into the common law of England, it ensured (in principle at least) legal protections and legal rights to all free men of England, regardless of social status. And in so far as that extension of rights was rooted in egalitarian principles, it was rooted in a shifting theological landscape that was coming to recognise the fundamental equality of the human persons.

# chapter three – references

1   Quoted in Larry Siedentop, *Inventing the Individual: The Origins of Western Liberalism*, (London: Allen Lane, 2014), p. 214.

2   See James Whitman, *The Origins of Reasonable Doubt: Theological Roots of the Criminal Trial* (London: Yale University Press, 2008), pp. 52–59.

3   Ibid, p. 57.

4   Ibid, p. 47.

5   Ibid, p. 48.

6   See Baldwin, "Master Stephen Langton" pp. 811–823.

7   Ibid, p. 818 (emphasis mine).

8   Ibid, p. 813. See also D'Avray, "Magna Carta", p. 429.

9   See 1 Samuel 10:24-25.

10  Baldwin, "Master Stephen Langton", p. 813.

11  Charles McIlwain, "Due Process of Law in the Magna Carta" in *Columbia Law Review*, Vol. 14, No. 1 (January 1914), p. 37.

12  See Holt, *Magna Carta*, pp. 78–80.

13  See John of Salisbury, *Policraticus: Of the Frivolities of Courtiers and the Footprints of Philosophers*, ed. and trans. Cary Nederman (Cambridge: Cambridge University Press, 2006), pp. 27–63.

14  Here, John of Salisbury pre-empts Stephen Langton, suggesting that in carrying out judgement according to the law, it is the law (rather than the king) which condemns the guilty party – the implication being that the king is thus excused of responsibility for the execution. (See Ibid, p. 31 – "it is the aim of [the king's] duties to strike down whoever the law adjudges must be struck down" and "[the king] may frequently kill and still not be a man of blood nor incur the accusation of murder or crime".)

15  Ibid, p. 28.

16  Ibid, p. 25.

17  Ibid, pp. 28–29.

18  Ibid, p. 30.

19  Brian Tierney, *Religion, law, and the growth of constitutional thought 1150–1650* (Cambridge: Cambridge University Press, 1982), p. 18.

20  Natalie Fryde, *Why Magna Carta? Angevin England revisited* (Munster: LIT, 2001) pp .109–111.

21  Nederman, "The Liberty of the Church", p. 457.

22  Holt, *Magna Carta*, pp. 277–278.

23  Quoted in Jean Porter, "Custom, Ordinance and Natural Right in Gratian's Decretum" in The Nature of Customary Law, ed. A. Perreau-Saussine and J. Murphy (Cambridge: Cambridge

University Press, 2007), p. 79 (In the above quote, I have changed the translation of the word *ius* from "right" to "law", to avoid confusion with other works).

24   Siedentop, *Inventing the Individual*, p. 216.

25   Ibid, p. 218.

26   Aside from Siedentop, *Inventing the Individual*, see: Nicholas Wolterstorff, *Justice: Rights and Wrongs* (Princeton: Princeton University Press, 2008) and Brian Tierney, *The Idea of Natural Rights*, (Grand Rapids: Wm. B. Eerdmans Publishing, 2001).

27   Tierney, *Natural Rights*, p. 70.

28   Ibid, pp. 70–71.

29   See Wolterstorff, *Justice*, pp. 59–132.

# conclusion

It's a common criticism coming from academic quarters that the public perception of the Magna Carta illustrates a sharp disconnect with its political reality. This is a document which pitted one pillar of the establishment against another; a document whose authors remained deeply committed to many of the basic precepts and hierarchies upon which the medieval social order was established. It was no manifesto for revolution. Many of the barons (and indeed bishops) who were involved in its formation would be horrified to learn of the causes to which it has been adopted over the centuries – from rebellion against the Stuart monarchy in the 17th century, to the Universal Declaration on Human Rights in the 20th.

> *As successive generations have read their own concerns and desires into its text, so the Magna Carta has developed as a document of legend and myth – foisted with a concept of liberty to which its authors would never have acceded.*

There is probably some truth in this line of reasoning. Where we have, historically speaking, looked to the Magna Carta to support modern notions of inherent human rights or democratic authority, we have tended to use a version that has been greatly distorted by the reflection of history. As successive generations have read their own concerns and desires into its text, so the Magna Carta has developed as a document of legend and myth – foisted with a concept of liberty to which its authors would never have acceded.

And yet it is also true that this mythological version of the Magna Carta did not emerge out of thin air. Despite its origins in the self-interest of an elite, the Great Charter of the Liberties of England *does* contain ideas that, in their own time and their own place, were deeply radical. We have discussed the most salient ideas in this essay – ideas concerning the central role of due process, the legitimation of arbitration in the affairs of the king, and the extension of rights language to all free men. These libertarian notions might not have formed the primary focus of baronial demands, but they are present nevertheless, giving the specific demands a basic structure and direction. The fact that these principles have become the central focus of a "Magna Carta mythology" does not negate their existence in the original document.

What this essay has attempted to show is that these principles outlined above, present in the Magna Carta at its very inception and fleshed out and emphasised in the centuries since, are principles that were themselves rooted in the developments of Christian theology. Moreover, their appearance in the Magna Carta, and indeed their preservation in the Magna Carta down the centuries, is indebted to the influence of the Christian Church and the Archbishop of Canterbury, Stephen Langton. If the Magna Carta is, as Lord Denning once suggested, the "foundation of the freedom of the individual against the arbitrary authority of the despot", it occupies this place in history only because the Church gave it the required intellectual and practical tools – from the ideas that shaped it, to the practical support of an established body with considerable political authority. Without the support of the Church, and without the theological developments which provided the Magna Carta's authors with their intellectual framework, it is doubtful whether 2015 would be remembered as the 800th anniversary of anything of particular note.

When we come to celebrate the history of the Magna Carta then, we should not forget the contribution of the Christian Church. We should not bow to the notion that the Magna Carta is a product of nothing more than selfish intent. Certainly, practical self-interest was a vital contributing factor to its development. But modern historical study is all-too ready to ignore the contribution of ideas to the shaping of history – especially ideas that come with a Christian bent. Given how vital theological and philosophical developments have been in shaping the way we as a nation have historically thought and responded, this is a mistake. While it is true that ideas should not be treated in isolation from the practical demands which give them substance, neither should these practical demands be isolated from the ideas which shape and direct them. As the Magna Carta illustrates so perfectly, the particular developments of history require the more general ideas that frame their content.

*Magna Carta, then, deserves to be remembered as a document shaped by the history of religious thought, just as much as it is remembered as an expression of secular demands.*

Magna Carta, then, deserves to be remembered as a document shaped by the history of religious thought, just as much as it is remembered as an expression of secular demands. And in so far as it represents a contribution to the evolution in political thought about the liberty of the individual and the limitations of the state, it is a decidedly Christian contribution. A contribution wrought in Christian theology, ecclesial law, and the sometimes murky world of Church politics.

# appendix

## the Magna Carta (1215)

*The following is a translation (with slight adaptions) of the 1215 Magna Carta, made available by the British Library[1] for reproduction under the Creative Commons Licence.[2]*

JOHN, by the grace of God King of England, Lord of Ireland, Duke of Normandy and Aquitaine, and Count of Anjou, to his archbishops, bishops, abbots, earls, barons, justices, foresters, sheriffs, stewards, servants, and to all his officials and loyal subjects, Greeting.

KNOW THAT BEFORE GOD, for the health of our soul and those of our ancestors and heirs, to the honour of God, the exaltation of the holy Church, and the better ordering of our kingdom, at the advice of our reverend fathers Stephen, archbishop of Canterbury, primate of all England, and cardinal of the holy Roman Church, Henry archbishop of Dublin, William bishop of London, Peter bishop of Winchester, Jocelin bishop of Bath and Glastonbury, Hugh bishop of Lincoln, Walter bishop of Worcester, William bishop of Coventry, Benedict bishop of Rochester, Master Pandulf subdeacon and member of the papal household, Brother Aymeric master of the knighthood of the Temple in England, William Marshal earl of Pembroke, William earl of Salisbury, William earl of Warren, William earl of Arundel, Alan of Galloway constable of Scotland, Warin fitz Gerald, Peter fitz Herbert, Hubert de Burgh seneschal of Poitou, Hugh de Neville, Matthew fitz Herbert, Thomas Basset, Alan Basset, Philip Daubeny, Robert de Roppeley, John Marshal, John fitz Hugh, and other loyal subjects:

(1) FIRST, THAT WE HAVE GRANTED TO GOD, and by this present charter have confirmed for us and our heirs in perpetuity, that the English Church shall be free, and shall have its rights undiminished, and its liberties unimpaired. That we wish this so to be observed, appears from the fact that of our own free will, before the outbreak of the present dispute between us and our barons, we granted and confirmed by charter the freedom of the Church's elections – a right reckoned to be of the greatest necessity and importance to it - and caused this to be confirmed by Pope Innocent III. This freedom we shall observe ourselves, and desire to be observed in good faith by our heirs in perpetuity.

TO ALL FREE MEN OF OUR KINGDOM we have also granted, for us and our heirs for ever, all the liberties written out below, to have and to keep for them and their heirs, of us and our heirs:

(2) If any earl, baron, or other person that holds lands directly of the Crown, for military service, shall die, and at his death his heir shall be of full age and owe a 'relief', the heir shall have his inheritance on payment of the ancient scale of 'relief'. That is to say, the heir or heirs of an earl shall pay £100 for the entire earl's barony, the heir or heirs of a knight £5 at most for the entire knight's 'fee', and any man that owes less shall pay less, in accordance with the ancient usage of 'fees'.

(3) But if the heir of such a person is under age and a ward, when he comes of age he shall have his inheritance without 'relief' or fine.

(4) The guardian of the land of an heir who is under age shall take from it only reasonable revenues, customary dues, and feudal services. He shall do this without destruction or damage to men or property. If we have given the guardianship of the land to a sheriff, or to any person answerable to us for the revenues, and he commits destruction or damage, we will exact compensation from him, and the land shall be entrusted to two worthy and prudent men of the same 'fee', who shall be answerable to us for the revenues, or to the person to whom we have assigned them. If we have given or sold to anyone the guardianship of such land, and he causes destruction or damage, he shall lose the guardianship of it, and it shall be handed over to two worthy and prudent men of the same 'fee', who shall be similarly answerable to us.

(5) For so long as a guardian has guardianship of such land, he shall maintain the houses, parks, fish preserves, ponds, mills, and everything else pertaining to it, from the revenues of the land itself. When the heir comes of age, he shall restore the whole land to him, stocked with plough teams and such implements of husbandry as the season demands and the revenues from the land can reasonably bear.

(6) Heirs may be given in marriage, but not to someone of lower social standing. Before a marriage takes place, it shall be made known to the heir's next-of-kin.

(7) At her husband's death, a widow may have her marriage portion and inheritance at once and without trouble. She shall pay nothing for her dower, marriage portion, or any inheritance that she and her husband held jointly on the day of

his death. She may remain in her husband's house for forty days after his death, and within this period her dower shall be assigned to her.

(8) No widow shall be compelled to marry, so long as she wishes to remain without a husband. But she must give security that she will not marry without royal consent, if she holds her lands of the Crown, or without the consent of whatever other lord she may hold them of.

(9) Neither we nor our officials will seize any land or rent in payment of a debt, so long as the debtor has movable goods sufficient to discharge the debt. A debtor's sureties shall not be distrained upon so long as the debtor himself can discharge his debt. If, for lack of means, the debtor is unable to discharge his debt, his sureties shall be answerable for it. If they so desire, they may have the debtor's lands and rents until they have received satisfaction for the debt that they paid for him, unless the debtor can show that he has settled his obligations to them.

(10) If anyone who has borrowed a sum of money from Jews dies before the debt has been repaid, his heir shall pay no interest on the debt for so long as he remains under age, irrespective of whom he holds his lands. If such a debt falls into the hands of the Crown, it will take nothing except the principal sum specified in the bond.

(11) If a man dies owing money to Jews, his wife may have her dower and pay nothing towards the debt from it. If he leaves children that are under age, their needs may also be provided for on a scale appropriate to the size of his holding of lands. The debt is to be paid out of the residue, reserving the service due to his feudal lords. Debts owed to persons other than Jews are to be dealt with similarly.

(12) No 'scutage' or 'aid' may be levied in our kingdom without its general consent, unless it is for the ransom of our person, to make our eldest son a knight, and (once) to marry our eldest daughter. For these purposes only a reasonable 'aid' may be levied. 'Aids' from the city of London are to be treated similarly.

(13) The city of London shall enjoy all its ancient liberties and free customs, both by land and by water. We also will and grant that all other cities, boroughs, towns, and ports shall enjoy all their liberties and free customs.

(14) To obtain the general consent of the realm for the assessment of an 'aid' - except in the three cases specified above - or a 'scutage', we will cause the archbishops,

bishops, abbots, earls, and greater barons to be summoned individually by letter. To those who hold lands directly of us we will cause a general summons to be issued, through the sheriffs and other officials, to come together on a fixed day (of which at least forty days notice shall be given) and at a fixed place. In all letters of summons, the cause of the summons will be stated. When a summons has been issued, the business appointed for the day shall go forward in accordance with the resolution of those present, even if not all those who were summoned have appeared.

(15) In future we will allow no one to levy an 'aid' from his free men, except to ransom his person, to make his eldest son a knight, and (once) to marry his eldest daughter. For these purposes only a reasonable 'aid' may be levied.

(16) No man shall be forced to perform more service for a knight's 'fee', or other free holding of land, than is due from it.

(17) Ordinary lawsuits shall not follow the royal court around, but shall be held in a fixed place.

(18) Inquests of novel disseisin, mort d'ancestor, and darrein presentment shall be taken only in their proper county court. We ourselves, or in our absence abroad our chief justice, will send two justices to each county four times a year, and these justices, with four knights of the county elected by the county itself, shall hold the assizes in the county court, on the day and in the place where the court meets.

(19) If any assizes cannot be taken on the day of the county court, as many knights and freeholders shall afterwards remain behind, of those who have attended the court, as will suffice for the administration of justice, having regard to the volume of business to be done.

(20) For a trivial offence, a free man shall be fined only in proportion to the degree of his offence, and for a serious offence correspondingly, but not so heavily as to deprive him of his livelihood. In the same way, a merchant shall be spared his merchandise, and a villein the implements of his husbandry, if they fall upon the mercy of a royal court. None of these fines shall be imposed except by the assessment on oath of reputable men of the neighbourhood.

(21) Earls and barons shall be fined only by their peers, and in proportion to the gravity of their offence.

(22) A fine imposed upon the lay property of a clerk in holy orders shall be assessed upon the same principles, without reference to the value of his ecclesiastical benefice.

(23) No town or person shall be forced to build bridges over rivers except those with an ancient obligation to do so.

(24) No sheriff, constable, coroners, or other royal officials are to hold lawsuits that should be held by the royal justices.

(25) Every county, hundred, wapentake, and tithing shall remain at its ancient rent, without increase, except the royal demesne manors.

(26) If at the death of a man who holds a lay 'fee' of the Crown, a sheriff or royal official produces royal letters patent of summons for a debt due to the Crown, it shall be lawful for them to seize and list movable goods found in the lay 'fee' of the dead man to the value of the debt, as assessed by worthy men. Nothing shall be removed until the whole debt is paid, when the residue shall be given over to the executors to carry out the dead man's will. If no debt is due to the Crown, all the movable goods shall be regarded as the property of the dead man, except the reasonable shares of his wife and children.

(27) If a free man dies intestate, his movable goods are to be distributed by his next-of-kin and friends, under the supervision of the Church. The rights of his debtors are to be preserved.

(28) No constable or other royal official shall take corn or other movable goods from any man without immediate payment, unless the seller voluntarily offers postponement of this.

(29) No constable may compel a knight to pay money for castle-guard if the knight is willing to undertake the guard in person, or with reasonable excuse to supply some other fit man to do it. A knight taken or sent on military service shall be excused from castle-guard for the period of this service.

(30) No sheriff, royal official, or other person shall take horses or carts for transport from any free man, without his consent.

(31) Neither we nor any royal official will take wood for our castle, or for any other purpose, without the consent of the owner.

(32) We will not keep the lands of people convicted of felony in our hand for longer than a year and a day, after which they shall be returned to the lords of the 'fees' concerned.

(33) All fish-weirs shall be removed from the Thames, the Medway, and throughout the whole of England, except on the sea coast.

(34) The writ called precipe shall not in future be issued to anyone in respect of any holding of land, if a free man could thereby be deprived of the right of trial in his own lord's court.

(35) There shall be standard measures of wine, ale, and corn (the London quarter), throughout the kingdom. There shall also be a standard width of dyed cloth, russet, and haberject, namely two ells within the selvedges. Weights are to be standardised similarly.

(36) In future nothing shall be paid or accepted for the issue of a writ of inquisition of life or limbs. It shall be given gratis, and not refused.

(37) If a man holds land of the Crown by 'fee-farm', 'socage', or 'burgage', and also holds land of someone else for knight's service, we will not have guardianship of his heir, nor of the land that belongs to the other person's 'fee', by virtue of the 'fee-farm', 'socage', or 'burgage', unless the 'fee-farm' owes knight's service. We will not have the guardianship of a man's heir, or of land that he holds of someone else, by reason of any small property that he may hold of the Crown for a service of knives, arrows, or the like.

(38) In future no official shall place a man on trial upon his own unsupported statement, without producing credible witnesses to the truth of it.

(39) No free man shall be seized or imprisoned, or stripped of his rights or possessions, or outlawed or exiled, or deprived of his standing in any way, nor will we proceed with force against him, or send others to do so, except by the lawful judgment of his peers or by the law of the land.

(40) To no one will we sell, to no one deny or delay right or justice.

(41) All merchants may enter or leave England unharmed and without fear, and may stay or travel within it, by land or water, for purposes of trade, free from all illegal exactions, in accordance with ancient and lawful customs. This, however, does not apply in time of war to merchants from a country that is at war with us. Any such merchants found in our country at the outbreak of war shall be detained

without injury to their persons or property, until we or our chief justice have discovered how our own merchants are being treated in the country at war with us. If our own merchants are safe they shall be safe too.

(42) In future it shall be lawful for any man to leave and return to our kingdom unharmed and without fear, by land or water, preserving his allegiance to us, except in time of war, for some short period, for the common benefit of the realm. People that have been imprisoned or outlawed in accordance with the law of the land, people from a country that is at war with us, and merchants - who shall be dealt with as stated above - are excepted from this provision.

(43) If a man holds lands of any 'escheat' such as the 'honour' of Wallingford, Nottingham, Boulogne, Lancaster, or of other 'escheats' in our hand that are baronies, at his death his heir shall give us only the 'relief' and service that he would have made to the baron, had the barony been in the baron's hand. We will hold the 'escheat' in the same manner as the baron held it.

(44) People who live outside the forest need not in future appear before the royal justices of the forest in answer to general summonses, unless they are actually involved in proceedings or are sureties for someone who has been seized for a forest offence.

(45) We will appoint as justices, constables, sheriffs, or other officials, only men that know the law of the realm and are minded to keep it well.

(46) All barons who have founded abbeys, and have charters of English kings or ancient tenure as evidence of this, may have guardianship of them when there is no abbot, as is their due.

(47) All forests that have been created in our reign shall at once be disafforested. River-banks that have been enclosed in our reign shall be treated similarly.

(48) All evil customs relating to forests and warrens, foresters, warreners, sheriffs and their servants, or river-banks and their wardens, are at once to be investigated in every county by twelve sworn knights of the county, and within forty days of their enquiry the evil customs are to be abolished completely and irrevocably. But we, or our chief justice if we are not in England, are first to be informed.

(49) We will at once return all hostages and charters delivered up to us by Englishmen as security for peace or for loyal service.

(50) We will remove completely from their offices the kinsmen of Gerard de Athée, and in future they shall hold no offices in England. The people in question are Engelard de Cigogné, Peter, Guy, and Andrew de Chanceaux, Guy de Cigogné, Geoffrey de Martigny and his brothers, Philip Marc and his brothers, with Geoffrey his nephew, and all their followers.

(51) As soon as peace is restored, we will remove from the kingdom all the foreign knights, bowmen, their attendants, and the mercenaries that have come to it, to its harm, with horses and arms.

(52) To any man whom we have deprived or dispossessed of lands, castles, liberties, or rights, without the lawful judgment of his peers, we will at once restore these. In cases of dispute the matter shall be resolved by the judgment of the twenty-five barons referred to below in the clause for securing the peace (§61). In cases, however, where a man was deprived or dispossessed of something without the lawful judgment of his peers by our father King Henry or our brother King Richard, and it remains in our hands or is held by others under our warranty, we shall have respite for the period commonly allowed to Crusaders, unless a lawsuit had been begun, or an enquiry had been made at our order, before we took the Cross as a Crusader. On our return from the Crusade, or if we abandon it, we will at once render justice in full.

(53) We shall have similar respite in rendering justice in connexion with forests that are to be disafforested, or to remain forests, when these were first afforested by our father Henry or our brother Richard; with the guardianship of lands in another person's 'fee', when we have hitherto had this by virtue of a 'fee' held of us for knight's service by a third party; and with abbeys founded in another person's 'fee', in which the lord of the 'fee' claims to own a right. On our return from the Crusade, or if we abandon it, we will at once do full justice to complaints about these matters.

(54) No one shall be arrested or imprisoned on the appeal of a woman for the death of any person except her husband.

(55) All fines that have been given to us unjustly and against the law of the land, and all fines that we have exacted unjustly, shall be entirely remitted or the matter decided by a majority judgment of the twenty-five barons referred to below in the clause for securing the peace (§61) together with Stephen, archbishop of Canterbury, if he can be present, and such others as he wishes to bring with him. If the archbishop cannot be present, proceedings shall continue without him, provided that if any of the twenty-five barons has been involved in a similar suit

himself, his judgment shall be set aside, and someone else chosen and sworn in his place, as a substitute for the single occasion, by the rest of the twenty-five.

(56) If we have deprived or dispossessed any Welshmen of land, liberties, or anything else in England or in Wales, without the lawful judgment of their peers, these are at once to be returned to them. A dispute on this point shall be determined in the Marches by the judgment of peers. English law shall apply to holdings of land in England, Welsh law to those in Wales, and the law of the Marches to those in the Marches. The Welsh shall treat us and ours in the same way.

(57) In cases where a Welshman was deprived or dispossessed of anything, without the lawful judgment of his peers, by our father King Henry or our brother King Richard, and it remains in our hands or is held by others under our warranty, we shall have respite for the period commonly allowed to Crusaders, unless a lawsuit had been begun, or an enquiry had been made at our order, before we took the Cross as a Crusader. But on our return from the Crusade, or if we abandon it, we will at once do full justice according to the laws of Wales and the said regions.

(58) We will at once return the son of Llywelyn, all Welsh hostages, and the charters delivered to us as security for the peace.

(59) With regard to the return of the sisters and hostages of Alexander, king of Scotland, his liberties and his rights, we will treat him in the same way as our other barons of England, unless it appears from the charters that we hold from his father William, formerly king of Scotland, that he should be treated otherwise. This matter shall be resolved by the judgment of his peers in our court.

(60) All these customs and liberties that we have granted shall be observed in our kingdom in so far as concerns our own relations with our subjects. Let all men of our kingdom, whether clergy or laymen, observe them similarly in their relations with their own men.

(61) SINCE WE HAVE GRANTED ALL THESE THINGS for God, for the better ordering of our kingdom, and to allay the discord that has arisen between us and our barons, and since we desire that they shall be enjoyed in their entirety, with lasting strength, for ever, we give and grant to the barons the following security:

The barons shall elect twenty-five of their number to keep, and cause to be observed with all their might, the peace and liberties granted and confirmed to them by this charter.

If we, our chief justice, our officials, or any of our servants offend in any respect against any man, or transgress any of the articles of the peace or of this security, and the offence is made known to four of the said twenty-five barons, they shall come to us - or in our absence from the kingdom to the chief justice - to declare it and claim immediate redress. If we, or in our absence abroad the chief justice, make no redress within forty days, reckoning from the day on which the offence was declared to us or to him, the four barons shall refer the matter to the rest of the twenty-five barons, who may distrain upon and assail us in every way possible, with the support of the whole community of the land, by seizing our castles, lands, possessions, or anything else saving only our own person and those of the queen and our children, until they have secured such redress as they have determined upon. Having secured the redress, they are to resume their normal obedience to us.

Any man who so desires may take an oath to obey the commands of the twenty-five barons for the achievement of these ends, and to join with them in assailing us to the utmost of his power. We give public and free permission to take this oath to any man who so desires, and at no time will we prohibit any man from taking it. Indeed, we will compel any of our subjects who are unwilling to take it to swear it at our command.

If one of the twenty-five barons dies or leaves the country, or is prevented in any other way from discharging his duties, the rest of them shall choose another baron in his place, at their discretion, who shall be duly sworn in as they were.

In the event of disagreement among the twenty-five barons on any matter referred to them for decision, the verdict of the majority present shall have the same validity as a unanimous verdict of the whole twenty-five, whether these were all present or some of those summoned were unwilling or unable to appear.

The twenty-five barons shall swear to obey all the above articles faithfully, and shall cause them to be obeyed by others to the best of their power.

We will not seek to procure from anyone, either by our own efforts or those of a third party, anything by which any part of these concessions or liberties might be revoked or diminished. Should such a thing be procured, it shall be null and void and we will at no time make use of it, either ourselves or through a third party.

(62) We have remitted and pardoned fully to all men any ill-will, hurt, or grudges that have arisen between us and our subjects, whether clergy or laymen, since the

beginning of the dispute. We have in addition remitted fully, and for our own part have also pardoned, to all clergy and laymen any offences committed as a result of the said dispute between Easter in the sixteenth year of our reign (i.e. 1215) and the restoration of peace.

In addition we have caused letters patent to be made for the barons, bearing witness to this security and to the concessions set out above, over the seals of Stephen archbishop of Canterbury, Henry archbishop of Dublin, the other bishops named above, and Master Pandulf.

(63) IT IS ACCORDINGLY OUR WISH AND COMMAND that the English Church shall be free, and that men in our kingdom shall have and keep all these liberties, rights, and concessions, well and peaceably in their fullness and entirety for them and their heirs, of us and our heirs, in all things and all places for ever.

Both we and the barons have sworn that all this shall be observed in good faith and without deceit. Witness the abovementioned people and many others.

Given by our hand in the meadow that is called Runnymede, between Windsor and Staines, on the fifteenth day of June in the seventeenth year of our reign.

# appendix – references

1    http://www.bl.uk/magna-carta/articles/magna-carta-english-translation

2    http://creativecommons.org/licenses/by/4.0/